Fairies

Adult Coloring Book

First edition: 2019

Thank you for purchasing this coloring book! I hope that you enjoy coloring it as much as I enjoyed creating it. Please consider leaving a review, I really appreciate hearing your opinion!

Sign-Up to Get a Free Coloring Book

Subscribe to our newsletter and get a free printable coloring book of some of our most popular illustrations. Plus you'll receive special offers, sneak peeks at new releases, and more. Visit us at **www.creativecoloring.co** for details.

We want to hear from you!

We hope you've enjoyed this coloring book and that is brings you many hours of fun, stress relief, and creativity. We'd love to see and share your creations.

Send us your ideas, suggestions, and finished artwork:

www.creativecoloring.co
facebook.com/creativecoloringpress
Instagram: @creativecoloringpress
Twitter: @creativecoloringpress

Bonus

Turn the page for bonus pages from some of our most popular coloring books.

SUGAR SKULL
COLORING BOOK

Cat Coloring Book

An Adult Coloring Book for Cat Lovers

CATS
M
XXXIII

Beautiful DRESSES

An Adult Coloring Book for Fashionistas

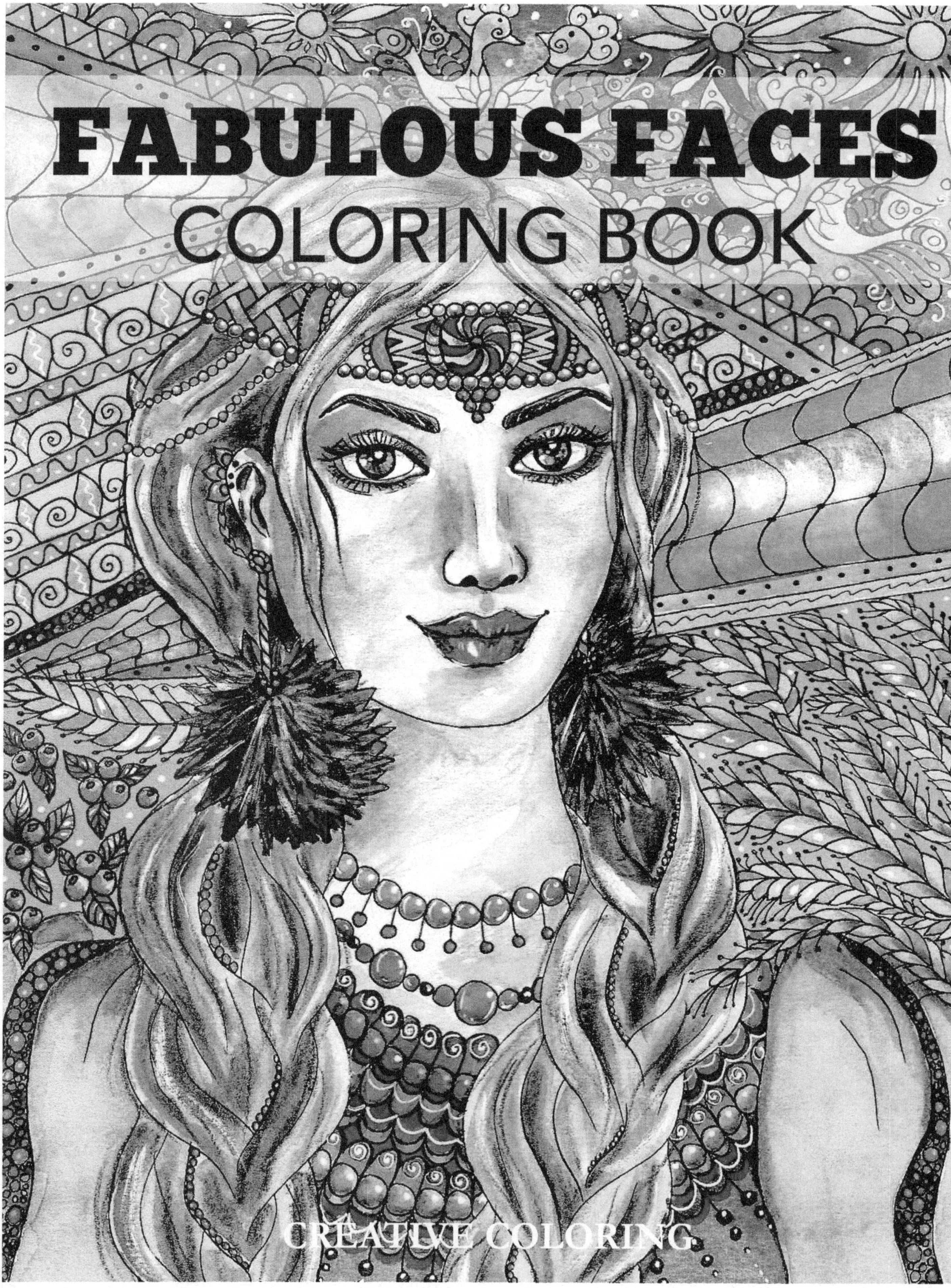
FABULOUS FACES
COLORING BOOK
CREATIVE COLORING

Made in the USA
Coppell, TX
10 January 2023

10630141R00057